D0519057

How Cats Conquered the World

Heather Hacking

Hodder & Stoughton
LONDON SYDNEY AUCKLAND

British Library Cataloguing in Publication Data
A record for this book is available from the British Library

ISBN 0 340 86321 8

Printed and bound in Great Britain by Clays Ltd, St Ives, plc

The paper and board used in this hardback are natural
recyclable products made from wood grown in sustainable
forests. The manufacturing processes conform to the
environmental regulations of the country of origin.

Hodder & Stoughton
A Division of Hodder Headline Ltd
338 Euston Road
London NW1 3BH

www.madaboutbooks.com

PART
ONE

Introduction

'It is a truth universally acknowledged that a man in possession of a warm house and a well-stocked fridge must be in want of a cat.'
Jane Austen, *Pride and Prejudice*.

It is also true that such a person had been observed and marked down as 'mine, all mine' by the said cat who had been stalking him for a while. This is part of a 'grand plan' adopted by all cats, from the dawn of time, to establish themselves as the dominant and, therefore, most comfortable species. To this day, most humans think they themselves are in control of all things earthly: this is a fancy that cats allow us to believe in because it would be too energetic and tiresome to battle it out hand-to-claw.

This book illustrates that the 'Big Bang' was just the sound of the first feline arriving through the cat-flap of time from a parallel universe that wasn't quite snug enough, and chronicles cats' ability from the cradle of civilisation to the present day to exert 'top claw'.

4

In the beginning, God was alone in the universe...

...well, not quite alone.

Two cats from the planet Mogg had spotted God...

...and thought that He might be a soft touch.

6

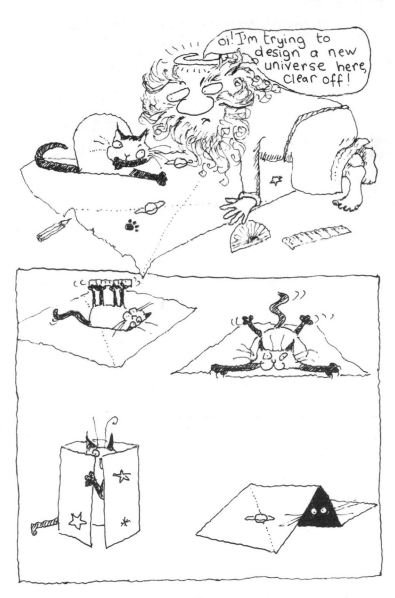

7

After an industrial dispute lasting six and a half centuries, a truce was reached and God got on with MIGHTY MATTERS.

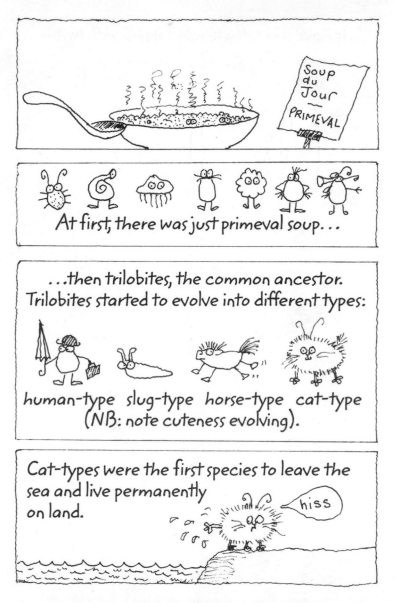

At first, there was just primeval soup...

...then trilobites, the common ancestor.
Trilobites started to evolve into different types:

human-type slug-type horse-type cat-type
(NB: note cuteness evolving).

Cat-types were the first species to leave the
sea and live permanently
on land.

hiss

10

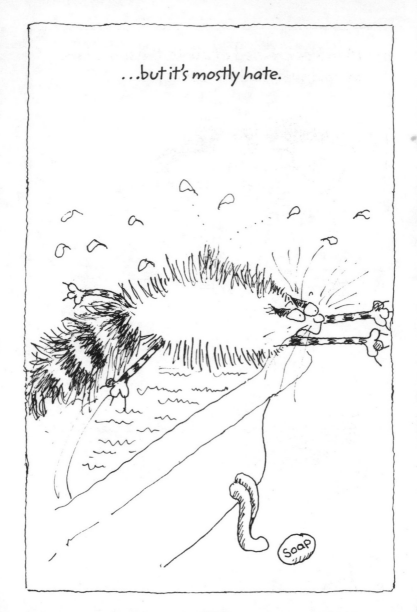

So, cats set about making themselves cute and indispensable.

We know this from cave paintings at Lascaux.

ANCIENT EGYPT
Hungry cats were having a tough time in the desert...

...as a result, they were thin, permanently hungry and a trifle moody — rather like jockeys and super models today.

Then... a visitor from Thebes.

Hey, chaps! You have got to see all the mice and sparrows in the granaries... and these Men-things who catch fish for you!!

peace!

16

So, in 2000 BC, the wild desert cats fluffed themselves up and blew into town.

17

19

CATS ARE GOOD MATHEMATICIANS

man + wheat + granary = mouse (× 10,000)

Early Egyptian flip chart.

Modern flip chart.

woman + ADYA shopping bag + nice semi-detached

BESTCO

cream Tibby

Cats were worshipped as goddesses.

Nothing has changed.

OUT OF EGYPT

CAT HYPNOSIS IN ANCIENT GREECE

Alexander the Great with his fine horse, Bucephalus, and his devoted cat, Ptibbles.

They were inseparable.

EARLY PERSIA

The horse-drawn carriage/mobile bed
was invented for King Darius I. It was
stuffed with silk cushions and
happy Persian cats.

If you need to locate hot water
pipes under floorboards, borrow some cats.

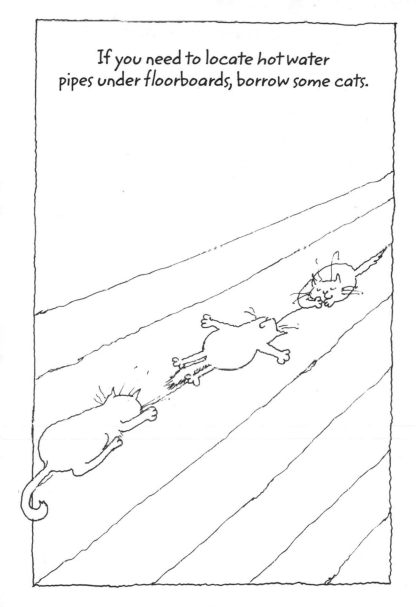

HADRIAN'S WALL

Just as Hadrian laid
the last dab of cement —
Glasgow One-Eye Wullie was sizing up
Middlesborough Mad Mick.

THE DARK AGES

The warmest place to be was a monastery.

Cats withdrew support for the Viking king, Cnut, when he started messing about with waves.

THE BAYEUX TAPESTRY

hic EST WHISKAS

hic EST SARDINE

NON AMUSI

Harold of England offers dinner to Aethelfrida and Aethelstan.

William of Normandy offers Snails in garlic to Miu-Miu and Michel.

William crowns Harold with a dish of snails

WILLIAM

WILLIAM TETCHY EST

THE MIDDLE AGES

Falcons were not the only companions on birding expeditions

Cats do not do any work themselves.

C'mon, c'mon.... there's rabbits in there...

Peasants cutting wheat, from "The Très Riches Heures du Duc de Furry"

Cats liked to hang around with witches
because they had the best fires...

...and there was usually a newt stew
on the go.

Distinctive medieval shoes amused cats for a while...

...then they took up banqueting.

Cats educated owners on what food was acceptable.

Since then cats have lavished every effort on food training.

...actually, I was hoping for salmon

Your supper, my Liege..

41

The Black Prince is being prepared for battle.

Joan of Arc hears voices.

MEDIEVAL ASIA

In outer Mongolia, there were herds of horses, fearless riders, cold winds, persistent snow, yak tea for supper and <u>no</u> cats.

no way!

Robert the Bruce was not inspired to victory by a spider.

TWO GREAT MYSTERIES SOLVED:
What made Mona Lisa smile?

Who taught Machiavelli to be devious?

HOW TO KILL SNEAKILY and QUIETLY

The Prints

THE SPANISH INQUISITION

49

CATS HAVE INFLUENCED WRITERS...

Henry the Navigator of Portugal was originally known as Henry the Embroiderer...

...until his cat decided to show him something.

Isambard Kingdom Brunel

ANCIENT CHINA

Cats went through a fairly unpopular period during the Ming Dynasty....

...and almost changed the storyline on Willow Pattern plates.

THE HOUSE OF ORANGE

The inseparable William-and-Mary and their cats...

...co-ruled Britain as 'William-and-Mary-and-Ted-and-Alice.'

WHO DROVE GEORGE III TO MADNESS?

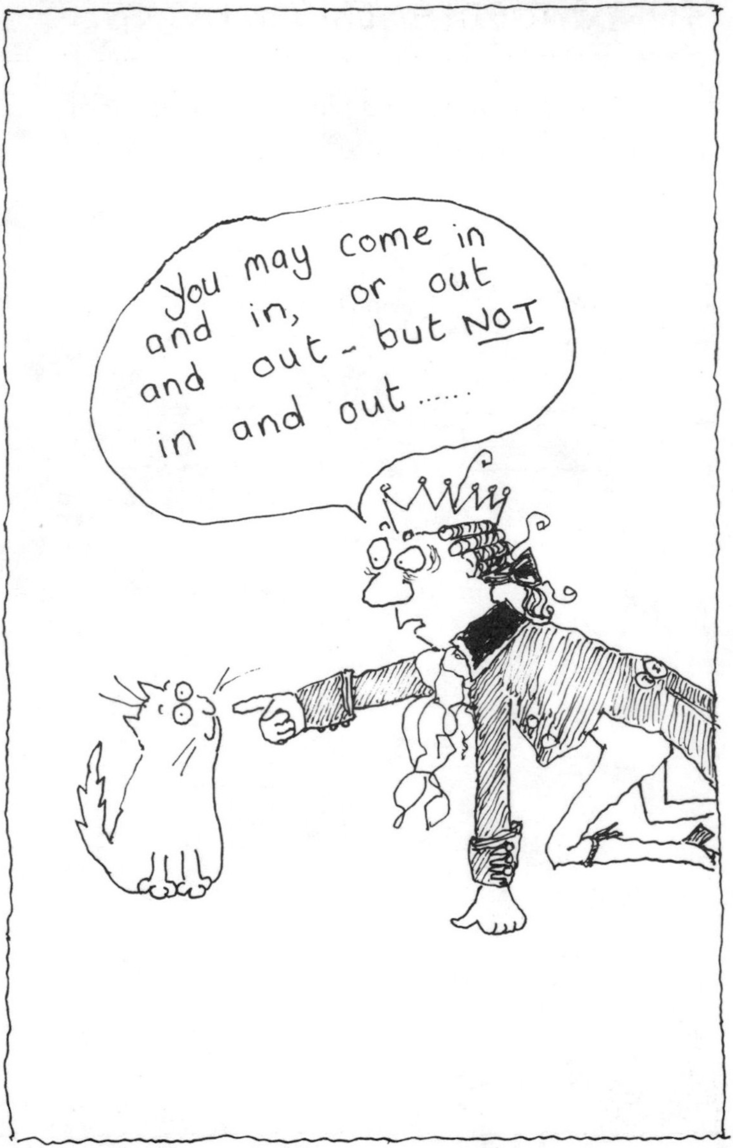
You may come in and in, or out and out - but NOT in and out......

THE AMERICAN WAR OF INDEPENDENCE

Why did George Washington cut down his father's cherry tree?

The Declaration of Independence

VICTORIAN BRITAIN

Prime Minister Disraeli and his cat, Dizzy,
persuade Queen Victoria (with her cat,
Queenie) to become Empress of India.

Cats have tried to get into the warmth and luxury of Buckingham Palace, but the Royal Family favour corgis. However, there are plans...

PART TWO

Cats don't always know what's best for them.

Cats can operate new gadgets, e.g. ordering on the internet.

me??
no, that wasn't me......

Cats have little respect for priceless china...

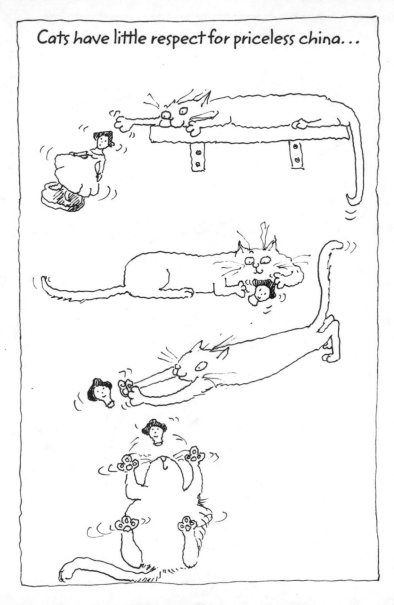

...pearl earrings, gold cufflinks,

sheer stockings,

antique necklaces,
or designer handbags.

Cats derive great comfort from exercising their claws...

...on cashmere sweaters...

...on expensive tights...

...on lambswool jumpers...

...and silk pyjamas.

If you are owned by a white cat...

...she would prefer you to wear black.

Conversely, your black cat...

...feels that he is making more of a mark in life if you wear white.

A CUTE-NESS DIAGRAM

bright, loving eyes in gemstone colours

swivelly ears turned to you

fluffy, expressive tail

incredibly velvety little nose

winning smile

tiny, harmless teeth

soft, gentle feet, no sign of hidden armoury

rear end bits discreetly upholstered with fur

tickle-able tummy

...can this be the same animal that you tried to get into the cat-carrier?

Cats will share a bed, but prefer to have the whole thing to themselves.

The attentive owner will provide several
bowls of fresh water

...which will be
studiously ignored.

Cats do not like their owner's attention to stray.

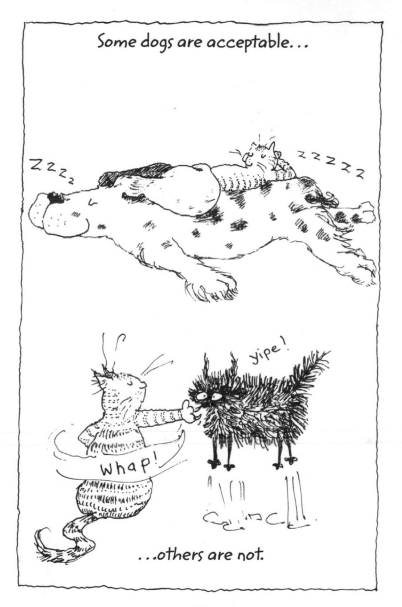

Cats love children...

...conquering them
is a pushover.

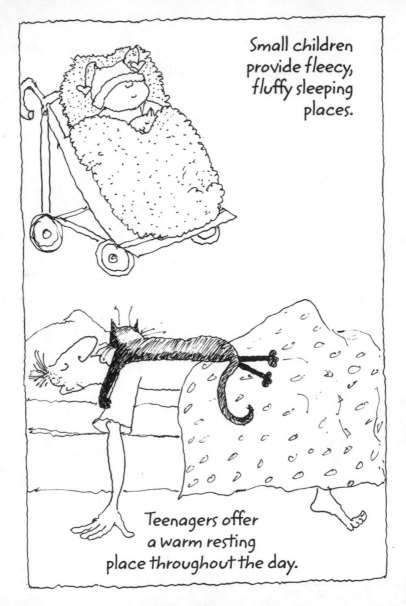

Small children provide fleecy, fluffy sleeping places.

Teenagers offer a warm resting place throughout the day.

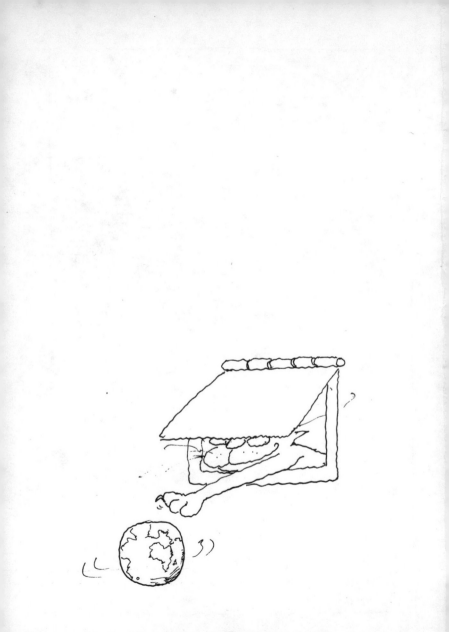